Our Solar System

Amanda Davis

The Rosen Publishing Group's
PowerKids Press™
New York

Published in 1997 by The Rosen Publishing Group, Inc.
29 East 21st Street, New York, NY 10010

First Edition

Book Design: Erin McKenna

Photo Credits: Cover and pp. 9, 16, 17 © NASA/FPG International Corp.; pp. 4, 8, 19, 20 © Telegraph Colour Library/FPG International Corp.; p. 7, 22, 23 © FPG International Corp.; p. 12 © Finley-Holiday/FPG International Corp.; p. 15 © Jack Zehrt/FPG International Corp.

Davis, Amanda
       Our Solar System / by Amanda Davis
            p.   cm. — (Exploring Space)
       Includes index.
       Summary: Briefly describes the sun, moon, and planets, as well as the force of gravity that connects them.
       ISBN 0-8239-5060-3
       1. Solar System—Juvenile literature. [1. Solar system.]
       I. Title. II. Series: Davis, Amanda. Exploring space.
       QB501.3.D39 1997
       523.2—dc21
                                                                                    96–53488
                                                                                        CIP
                                                                                         AC

Manufactured in the United States of America

Contents

What Is the Solar System?

The solar system is the part of the **universe** (YOO-nih-vers) that we live in. The sun, Earth, eight other planets, many moons, comets, and **asteroids** (AS-ter-oydz) are all parts of the solar system.

The word "solar" means anything having to do with the sun. The sun is the center of the solar system. All the other parts **revolve** (ree-VOLV) around it. The sun is much bigger than the other objects in the solar system. Our solar system is in the **galaxy** (GAL-ik-see) called the Milky Way.

◀ Everything in our solar system revolves around the sun, which is a giant star.

Where Did Our Solar System Come From?

Most **scientists** (SY-en-tists) agree that our solar system formed from a huge cloud of gas in space. About 4½ billion years ago, this gas cloud caved in on itself and formed a star.

The dust and gas left over after the star was made formed a huge disk around the star. Over a long period of time, the dust and gas in the disk formed the nine planets of our solar system.

The nine planets in our solar system are Mercury, Venus, Earth, Mars, Jupiter, Saturn, Uranus, Neptune, and Pluto.

Our solar system was formed from a cloud of gas that became a star, much like the stars in this star cluster. ▶

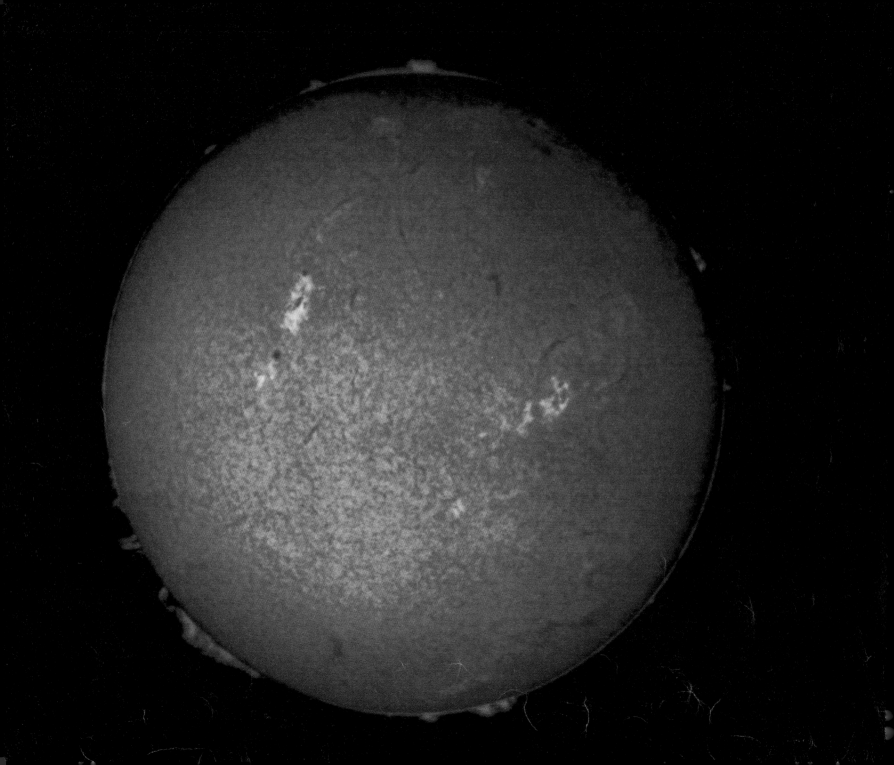

The Sun

The sun is a star. It doesn't look like a small bright dot in the sky like the other stars do. That's because it is so close to Earth. The sun is so big that almost 1½ million Earths could fit inside it!

The sun is a giant ball of very hot gases. The **temperature** (TEMP-rah-chur) at the core, or middle, of the sun is 27 million degrees! The temperature in Earth's hottest desert has never gone over 136 degrees.

◀ The temperature on the surface of
the sun is about 6,000 degrees.

Why Do the Planets Circle the Sun?

The sun's **gravity** (GRA-vih-tee) is very strong. This causes the planets to **orbit** (OR-bit), or circle, it.

Gravity is the natural **force** (FORSS) between all objects. This force causes objects to be attracted to each other. The more **massive** (MA-siv) an object is, the stronger its gravity.

Because the sun is the most massive object in the solar system, it has the strongest gravity. That's why the planets orbit the sun and not the other way around.

SPACE FACT

It takes Earth one year to travel around the sun. It takes Pluto, the farthest planet from the sun, almost 249 years to make the same trip!

Each planet in the solar system revolves on its own path around the sun. ▶

Orbits of the Planets

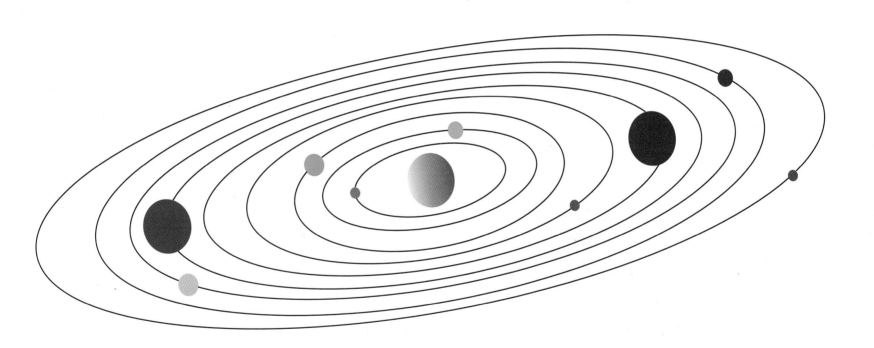

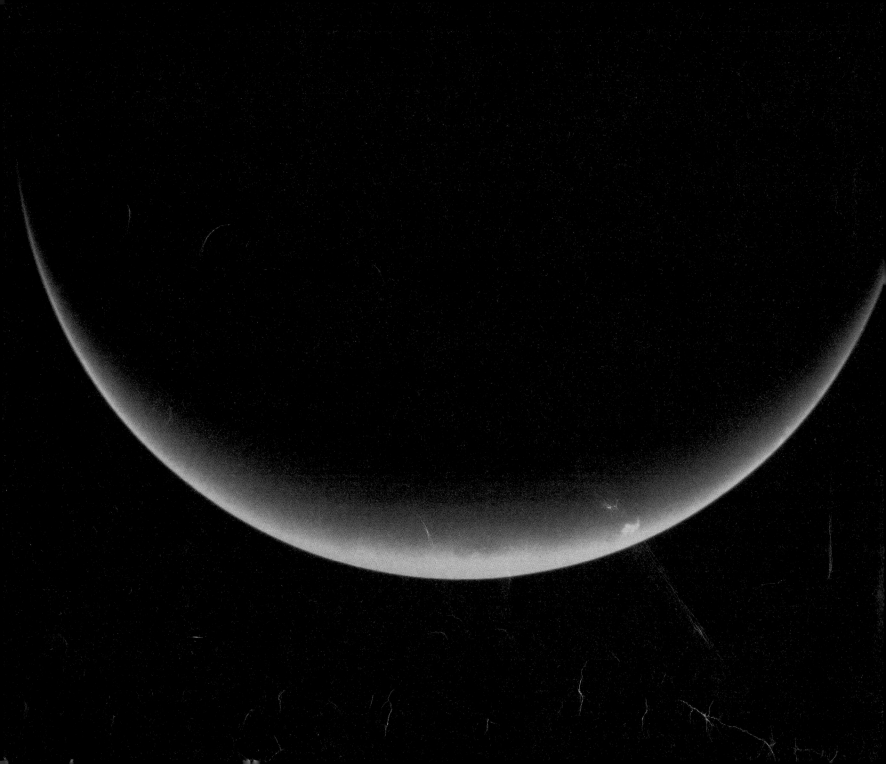

The Planets

Nine planets orbit the sun. Some are made of rock, like Earth. Others are made of gases. The planets began to form just after the sun formed.

Some of the planets can be seen from Earth just by looking at the right place in the sky. They look like very bright stars. But the light doesn't come from inside the planet, like a star's light does. The light is a **reflection** (ree-FLEK-shun) of the sun's light.

SPACE FACT

Planets often shine brighter than stars in the night sky. If something looks red, you might be looking at Mars. If it looks blue it might be Venus!

◀ Neptune's light comes from a reflection of the sun's light.

Solid Planets

The planets closest to the sun are solid like Earth. Mercury is much smaller than Earth and is the closest planet to the sun. Then comes Venus, which is the closest in size to Earth. Venus is completely covered by clouds.

We live on Earth, the third planet from the sun. The next planet is Mars. It has two moons. The other solid planet in the solar system is Pluto. It is the farthest planet from the sun. We don't know very much about this small planet.

Venus is the second closest planet to the sun. ▶

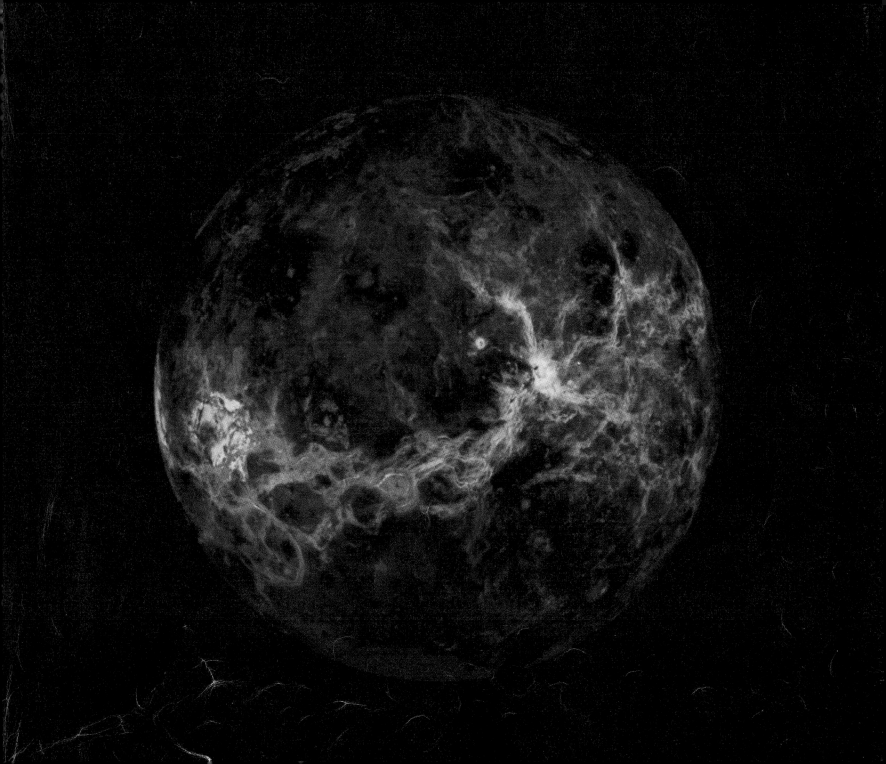

Gaseous Planets

The largest planets in the solar system are Saturn, Jupiter, Uranus, and Neptune. They are called **gaseous** (GA-shus) planets because they are made mostly of gases.

These planets don't have solid **surfaces** (SER-fiss-ez) like our planet does. Instead, their surfaces are made up of layers of clouds and gases. They all have rings made of dust and rocks. Saturn is famous for its beautiful rings.

Jupiter is known for its giant red spot. The red spot is a storm on Jupiter's surface. It was discovered in 1664 by a man named Robert Hooke. This huge, swirling storm is bigger than Earth.

◀ So far, scientists have discovered that Saturn has eighteen moons.

Earth

Earth, the planet we live on, is about 93 million miles from the sun. If there was a highway to the sun, it would take almost 163 years to drive there in a car!

Scientists believe that Earth is about 4½ billion years old.

The **atmosphere** (AT-mus-feer), or air, around our planet provides **oxygen** (AHK-sih-jen) for us to breathe. It also protects us from harmful heat and energy from the sun.

SPACE FACT Earth is the fifth largest planet. Jupiter is the largest planet and Pluto is the smallest.

It takes Earth 365¼ days to travel around the sun. ▶

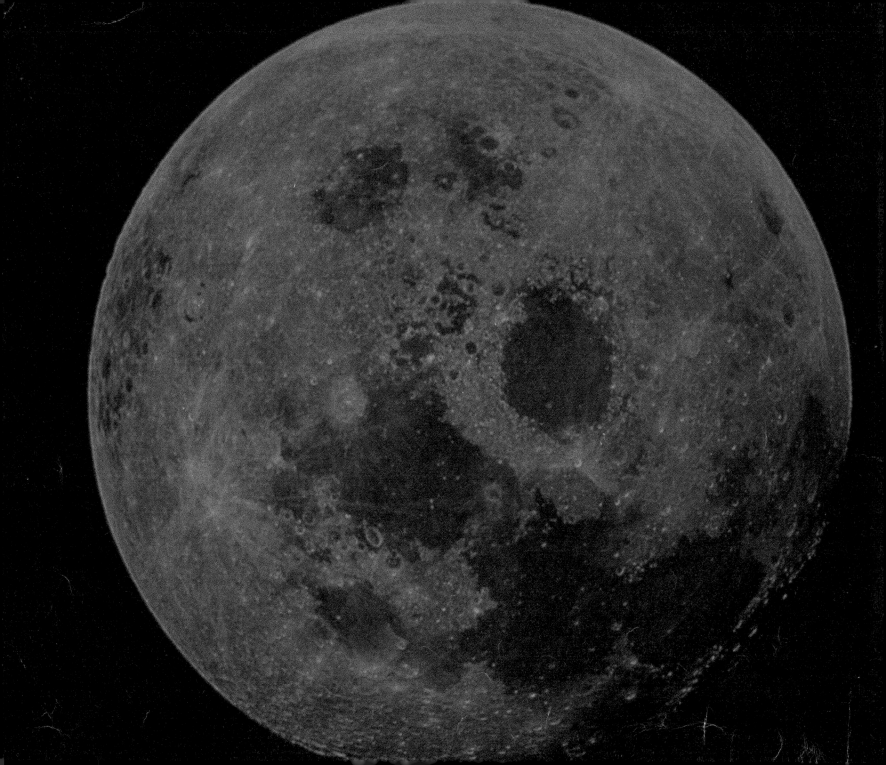

The Moon

The moon orbits Earth just like Earth orbits the sun.

On July 20, 1969, **astronauts** (AS-tro-notz) flew in a spaceship to the moon. They actually walked on the moon's surface and brought moon rocks back to Earth for scientists to study. The first person to walk on the moon was an astronaut named Neil Armstrong.

The moon has no atmosphere and its surface is marked by giant **craters** (KRAY-terz). Craters are made by asteroids that crashed on the moon.

◀ The moon's craters can be seen from Earth. They look like dark spots.

Other Solar Systems

Scientists believe there are many stars in the universe that have planets orbiting them like our sun does. That means there may be other solar systems besides ours in the universe.

In January 1996, scientists found two stars, each with a planet orbiting it. One star is called 70 Virginis. The planet orbiting this star is about nine times as big as Jupiter.

Scientists haven't found another planet like Earth. But they continue to look for more planets and more solar systems in the universe.

Glossary

asteroid (AS-ter-oyd) A rock that orbits other larger objects in space.

astronaut (AS-tro-not) A person who is trained to travel into space.

atmosphere (AT-mus-feer) The air surrounding some planets.

Charon (SHA-rin) Pluto's moon.

crater (KRAY-ter) A wide hole on the surface of a moon or planet where an asteroid hit it.

force (FORSS) Something in nature that causes action.

galaxy (GAL-ik-see) A large group of stars and the planets that circle them.

gaseous (GA-shus) Something made of gas; not liquid or solid.

gravity (GRA-vih-tee) A force between two objects that causes them to be attracted to each other.

massive (MA-siv) Something that is made up of a large amount of something else.

orbit (OR-bit) How something circles around something else.

oxygen (AHK-sih-jen) A kind of gas that is in the air. Humans need oxygen to breathe.

reflection (ree-FLEK-shun) An image created when light bounces off an object and shines in a different direction.

revolve (ree-VOLV) To move in a path around something.

scientist (SY-en-tist) A person who studies the way things are and act in the universe.

surface (SER-fiss) The top or outside of something.

temperature (TEMP-rah-chur) How hot or cold something is.

universe (YOO-nih-vers) Everything there is. Our solar system is just a small part of the universe.

Index